Blending Language Skills

SIMPLIFIED

Vocabulary, Grammar, and Writing

Book D
Grade 4

Author
Judith Sweeney
Early Childhood Specialist and Field Coordinator
Keystone College

Cover Design
David Justice

Cover Template
Elliot Kreloff, Inc.

Copy Editor
Juanita Galuska

Reviewer
Elizabeth Swartz

Edited by
Betsy Ochester

Margie Hayes Richmond, Director
Essential Learning Products

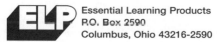 Essential Learning Products
P.O. Box 2590
Columbus, Ohio 43216-2590

A Division of Teachers' Publishing Group, a Highlights Company
Copyright ©2003 Essential Learning Products

Printed in China
10 9 8 7 6 5 4 3 2 1

CONTENTS

STANDARDS CORRELATION

The following IRA/NCTE standards are met throughout this book:
Refer to contents page for specific correlations for each lesson.

#3

Students apply a wide range of strategies to comprehend, interpret, evaluate, and appreciate texts. They draw on their prior experience, their interactions with other readers and writers, their knowledge of word meaning and of other texts, their word identification strategies, and their understanding of textual features (for example, sound-letter correspondence, sentence structure, context, graphics).

#4

Students adjust their use of spoken, written, and visual language (for example, conventions, style, vocabulary) to communicate effectively with a variety of audiences and for different purposes.

#5

Students employ a wide range of strategies as they write and use different writing-process elements appropriately to communicate with different audiences for a variety of purposes.

#6

Students apply knowledge of language structure, language conventions (for example, spelling and punctuation), media techniques, figurative language, and genre to create, critique, and discuss print and nonprint texts.

#7

Students conduct research on issues and interests by generating ideas and questions, and by posing problems. They gather, evaluate, and synthesize data from a variety of sources (for example, print and nonprint texts, artifacts, people) to communicate their discoveries in ways that suit their purpose and audience.

#12

Students use spoken, written, and visual language to accomplish their own purposes (for example, for learning, enjoyment, persuasion, and the exchange of information).

TEACHER'S GUIDE

Good basketball coaches have to teach players specific skills one by one. Players learn and practice how to dribble, make long shots, do lay-up shots, shoot free throws, and handle the ball with ease. Most players are better at some of these skills than others. But it is the players who can blend these skills into a strong overall performance who become champions. So it is with good teachers. Specific skills must be "taught in isolation," and then students need lots of opportunity to practice. Like basketball players, it is the students who can then blend and apply the skills that succeed.

The *Blending Language Skills Simplified* series will help students do just that. In each lesson, students can identify and practice a specific skill and then complete exercises that apply and blend those skills. The series' subtitle—*Vocabulary, Grammar, Writing*—-tells the rest of the story. These are the three elements of the lessons. Vocabulary is introduced and expanded in fun, creative ways. Grammar concepts that help build understanding of the structure of language are highlighted. And a variety of writing opportunities abound!

The many, many demands in today's skill-driven atmosphere often push aside the findings of child psychologist Piaget. He determined that because of how children's brains mature, they must be explicitly taught how concepts relate and connect. Using this book, students will see how vocabulary, grammar, and writing connect to build and enhance written and oral language skills. Lessons include other invaluable features, such as *off-the-page interactive* activities, *parent-involvement* ideas, and *journal-writing* suggestions.

Let's look at the format of each lesson:
Pre-Activity—These ideas set the stage for the lesson. Though not essential, the ideal approach would be for the teacher to present the directions and have students follow through in small or large groups. Most activities begin with a question that helps the students focus on a language concept and/or a specific theme. Students are then directed off the page to work on their own or with a friend.
Activity—This is the lesson's primary area for skill focus and practice. To better suit student modalities and eliminate boredom potential, the exercises vary in type, such as matching, coloring, drawing,

completion, writing sentences or short passages, and more. The majority of lessons also have exercises—some explicit and some open-ended—that call for more in-depth writing.
Post-Activity—These suggestions take the students off the page to apply what they've learned. They call for journal writing and/or are interactive. This is where many easy parent involvement ideas are presented.
Grammar Connection/Language Strategy/ Writing Tip—One of these features is presented as a call-out on every lesson. Short, simple explanations define the grammar concept of the lesson or state a tip or strategy that is applied in the lesson. The placing of this information "outside" the lesson proper gives the teacher flexibility on just how much to focus on it.
Extra—Just as the name implies, it is enriching and its use is optional. Students are encouraged to do research or are led to a higher level of thinking.

Two noteworthy features appear on pages 2 and 3:
Table of Contents—This page will be nearly indispensable in determining how and when to use specific lessons. Certainly, lessons can be used sequentially; they begin with the easiest and progress in difficulty within each book and throughout the series. However, this book offers more flexibility than most. The decision to use a lesson can be based on a *specific grammar concept*, a particular *kind of writing*, or on *cross-curricular thematic units*. All this information is right there on the Contents page.
Standards—A numbered list of the National Standards for English Language Arts is shown on page 3. The number of the standard(s) for each lesson is shown on the Contents page, making record-keeping a snap for busy teachers.

Are you a teacher who typically loves and depends on work sheets? If so, you'll appreciate the easy-to-use format and comprehensive skill content of this book. Or are you a teacher who only reluctantly embraces work-sheet use? If so, the creative, open-ended, off-the-page exercises will appeal to you. Developing a series of books that provides needed practice without stifling creativity and enthusiasm is the challenge that *Blending Language Skills Simplified* is intended to meet.

Grammar Connection

A *verb* is a word that shows action.

Extra

How many eggs are in a baker's dozen? Do you know why?

Pre-Activity

Have you ever visited a large farm? On a farm there are chores for everyone. Each day animals must be fed, plants watered, and crops harvested. Can you think of two other actions that have to be done on a farm?

Activity

A. On the Rich Ripe Fruit Farm, the peaches are ready for picking—and eating! Let's make a peach pie. Think about how to prepare dough for a piecrust. Match.

Step 1. combine   a. the dough

Step 2. add   b. flour and salt

Step 3. roll   c. into the baking tin

Step 4. press   d. off any extra dough

Step 5. trim   e. sugar and vanilla

B. Now that the dough is ready, it's time to add the peaches. Circle the verbs that describe what has to be done to the peaches before they go in the pie shell.

peel   throw   eat   core   slice   scratch

C. Write a few sentences that tell how to make a peach pie. Use some of the verbs from above.

_____

_____

_____

_____

_____

_____

Post-Activity

Look through some cookbooks with a family member. Find a recipe that looks good to you. Make it together. Eat and enjoy!

Pre-Activity

Can you picture three different types of trees? When we think of action words, we don't usually think of trees. Can you think of an action done by a tree? Does it grow? Can it bend?

Activity

A. When the seasons change, trees change, too. Some trees lose their leaves. They are called *deciduous* trees. Below is a list of actions for deciduous trees. Match the action to the season.

1. spring

2. summer

3. fall

4. winter

a. drop leaves, produce less food (chlorophyll)

b. bud, sprout, bloom, develop

c. stand bare, remain dormant (don't grow or reproduce)

d. thrive, flourish, store up food through photosynthesis

B. Underline the best action word for each sentence.

1. In the autumn, when the sun is less strong and the days are shorter, the stems of my leaves begin to decay and the leaves (rocket   drop   crash) to the ground.

2. During the long winter months, when the ground is frozen, I stay dormant and do not (grow   yell   complain) at all.

3. When the warm spring sun returns, my branches begin to (shake   sprout   shrink) and buds appear.

4. Summer is my favorite season because children play in me and my leaves (fall   fade   thrive) in the hot sun.

Grammar Connection

Verbs show action. Some actions, such as *grow* and *stand*, are not visible, yet they are still verbs.

C. Pretend you are a tree. Write a story about how it feels to change your looks so often. The first sentence is done for you. Underline each verb you use.

What a life! _____

_____

_____

_____

_____

_____

_____

_____

_____

_____

_____

D. Illustrate your story. Draw a picture of you as a tree!

Post-Activity

Find a book about trees. Then take a walk with a family member. See how many kinds of trees you can identify. Write the names in your journal. Can you describe what the trees are "doing" during this time of year?

Extra

I think that I shall never see a poem lovely as a tree.

The poet Joyce Kilmer wrote these lines. What do you think he meant by this? Do you agree with him? Why or why not? Try to find other poems about trees.

Pre-Activity

Do you know what this animal is? It is a bat. Most people find bats very interesting. What do you know about bats?

Activity

A. Read this paragraph. Then make a list of action words that describe the activities of bats.

The bat is the only mammal that can fly. A bat's body is furry and its wings are covered with smooth, flexible skin. Most species of bats live in attics, caves, or other dark, sheltered places. Some species live in trees. Bats are not seen very often because they roost in dark places and come out only at night, when most people are asleep. Bats search for insects to eat. Bats hang upside down when they are resting.

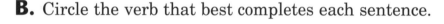

_____

_____

B. Circle the verb that best completes each sentence.

1. Bats (fly live) in sheltered places.

2. When most people are sleeping, bats are (sleeping flying).

3. Each night, bats (eat befriend) a large number of insects.

4. Although bats are harmless, many people (giggle scream) when they see one.

Post-Activity

Talk with a friend or family member about bats. Did either of you ever see one? Why not read books or watch videos to learn more about bats? Write about the experience in your journal.

Language Strategy

In many cultures, stories have been passed down from generation to generation. Instead of being written down, stories are told out loud. These stories are called *folktales*. Many of the folktales we know today come from this oral tradition.

Extra

Do you know the real reason why bats hang upside down? Research it.

Pre-Activity

Did you ever wonder why a pug dog has a flat nose or why pigs like to roll in the mud? In many cultures, there are special stories, such as "How the Elephant Got His Trunk," that explain everyday happenings. Do you know any stories like this?

Activity

Read this Laotian folktale. Then write a folktale of your own about bats. Use some of the verbs from the word box and some of your own.

Why Bat Hangs Upside Down

Bat thought he might be a bird. For a time, he flew happily with Bird. But when it came time to build a nest, he was too lazy. He told Bird, "Perhaps I am a rat. I'll go live with Rat." Bat and Rat had fun playing together until it came time to build a nest. That's when Bat changed his mind and decided to return to Bird. But she sent him back to Rat. Back and forth flew Bat until both Bird and Rat got tired of him. They said, "Bat, you're lazy. Since you can't decide whether to be a bird in the air or a rat on the ground, you can hang upside down between the sky and the earth." That's exactly what Bat did. To this day bats live in caves, hanging upside down. And because they don't want to meet Bird or Rat, they come out only at night to hunt for food.

taught	grip	clutch	defend	see	fly

_____

_____

_____

_____

_____

_____

Post-Activity

Read your folktale to a friend. Ask him or her to tell it to someone else. Then ask *that* person to tell it, and so on. Pretty soon, you will have created your own folktale.

Pre-Activity

Name a person you admire. Can you name that person's favorite thing? Where do think his or her favorite place is? Think about your favorite places to spend time. Perhaps you like your bedroom, a bench in a park, a roller coaster, or maybe even a classroom.

Activity

A. Animals have favorite places where they like to spend time, too. Match each animal below to its habitat, or the place where it lives.

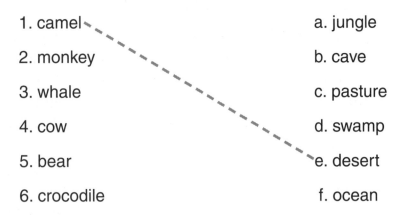

1. camel   a. jungle

2. monkey   b. cave

3. whale   c. pasture

4. cow   d. swamp

5. bear   e. desert

6. crocodile   f. ocean

B. Unscramble each group of letters to spell an animal name. Then write its habitat. Choose from the list above.

	Animal	Habitat
1. guinaa	*iguana*	*desert*
2. shero		
3. tba		
4. rahks		
5. lortagila		
6. pelehnat		

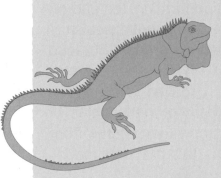

C. Choose one of the animals from page 10, or pick another favorite. Then find the answer to each question below. Answers should be nouns.

1. What are two things your animal likes to eat?

_____

2. In what country does your animal live?

_____

3. What is the animal's habitat?

_____

4. What activities does this animal do?

_____

_____

D. Now pretend you are a writer for a nature magazine. Your job is to travel to the animal's habitat and write a paragraph describing the animal. Use some of the nouns you wrote in Activity C.

_____

_____

_____

_____

_____

_____

_____

Extra

When you want to learn more about a topic, where do you look? Do you use a computer, read books, or watch videos?

Post-Activity

Play a game with a friend. Take turns pretending to be a certain animal. Give clues about the animal's habitat, diet, and so on. See how quickly your friend can figure out which animal it is.

Pre-Activity

Are you a student? a boy? a sister? a soccer player? a dancer? What name does your teacher call you? That is probably your proper name.

Activity

A. Match the proper nouns with the appropriate common noun for these famous people.

1.  Robert Fulton   a. author

2. Dwight Eisenhower   b. inventor

3. Laura Ingalls Wilder   c. artist

4. Louis Armstrong   d. president

5. Georgia O'Keefe   e. musician

B. List at least two more proper nouns for each of the common nouns.

1. author _____

_____

2. inventor _____

_____

3. artist _____

_____

4. president _____

_____

5. musician _____

_____

Post-Activity

Think about your family members. Include aunts, uncles, cousins, and grandparents. Write all their proper names in your journal. Write common nouns to tell who they are (such as girl or nephew). Do you have more proper nouns than common ones? Why?

Grammar Connection

A *noun* names a person, place, thing, or idea.

A *common noun* refers to general words, such as *teacher, town*, or *song*. Common nouns begin with lowercase letters.

A specific name, such as Mr. Timms or Wanda, is a *proper noun*. Proper nouns begin with capital letters.

Extra

Choose one of the people from Activity A. Read a bit about him or her. What places were important in her or his life? Is this a person you admire? Think about why or why not.

Grammar Connection

Specific place names, like those of countries and cities, are *proper nouns.*

Extra

Pick one of the above cities, countries, or oceans. Then look in a newspaper or online to find a local weather forecast. How does the weather there compare with your own?

Pre-Activity

Think about where you live. You probably have a street name, a town name, a county name, and a state name. Can you give the proper noun for each place? Now try it the other way. Can you give common nouns of proper nouns? For example, is the U.S.A. a state or a country? Is the Atlantic a desert or an ocean?

Activity

A. Here is a list of places. Write each proper noun under the correct common noun.

Toronto	Mexico	Pacific	San Francisco
Seattle	London	Antarctic	France
Indian	Argentina	U.S.A.	Tokyo
Atlantic	Arctic	China	

CITIES	COUNTRIES	OCEANS
_____	_____	_____
_____	_____	_____
_____	_____	_____
_____	_____	_____
_____	_____	_____

B. Which place would you most like to see? Write about it.

_____

_____

_____

_____

_____

_____

Post-Activity

Play a "Proper Name" game with family members. Name a common noun, such as *singers.* Then each of you list as many proper names of singers as you can.

Pre-Activity

Think of a noun. Was it a word you can "picture," such as a cat, a street, a barn, or a teacher? Some nouns can be tricky to picture. *Friendliness* and *honor* are two nouns that are hard to picture. Can you name a few more?

Activity

A. Complete each sentence with one of these "hard to see" nouns from the word bank.

> friendliness   accomplishment   ability
> permission   courage

1. Just finishing the race was a tremendous

   _____ for Ramal.

2. Shan seems to have natural athletic

   _____ .

3. It took great _____ to say no to the man's offer.

4. Anne needs _____ from her parents to enter the contest.

5. Ellen's _____ made the girls feel welcome.

B. Choose two of the words above and use them in sentences of your own.

_____

_____

_____

_____

Post-Activity

Courage and honesty are powerful ideas. A person who has these traits is most likely a remarkable human being. Together with a family member, try to think of a person you know who has these traits. Write about that person in your journal.

Grammar Connection

A *noun* is a person, place, thing, or idea. An *idea noun* can be a state of mind or a trait, like shyness or cowardice.

Extra

Can you think of three "hard to see" nouns that describe you?

Grammar Connection

Synonyms are words that have the same or nearly the same meaning.

Extra

How many synonyms can you think of for the word *work*? How about for *play*? Which word "wins"?

Pre-Activity

Think of a doctor. Now picture a physician. Did you imagine the same person? Words like *doctor* and *physician* are synonyms. Can you think of another synonym for doctor?

Activity

A. Match the synonyms.

1. career	a. performer
2. artist	b. attorney
3. teacher	c. sportsman
4. athlete	d. illustrator
5. accountant	e. builder
6. actor	f. author
7. carpenter	g. bookkeeper
8. lawyer	h. educator
9. writer	i. cook
10. chef	j. profession

B. Name three other careers. Can you think of at least one synonym for each?

Careers   Synonyms

_____ ➠ _____

_____ ➠ _____

_____ ➠ _____

Post-Activity

Choose an adult who has a career you'd like to know more about. Meet with him or her and ask questions about the job. (Be sure to come prepared with a few questions already thought out.) Write a paragraph about the career in your journal. Use synonyms if you can.

Pre-Activity

Read these sentences.

> The chubby dog walked across the lawn. As the pooch strolled, a fat cat ambled into the yard.

Can you identify four pairs of synonyms? One word in the sentence actually has two synonyms. What is it?

Activity

Find a synonym in the Wheel for each word below.

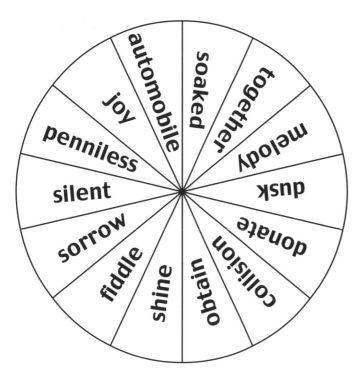

1. happiness _____
2. car _____
3. united _____
4. poor _____
5. wet _____
6. nightfall _____
7. quiet _____

8. tune _____
9. give _____
10. glow _____
11. get _____
12. crash _____
13. sadness _____
14. violin _____

Post-Activity

In your journal, continue the story of the cat and dog from the Pre-Activity. Can you include at least five synonyms from above?

Writing Tip

Using synonyms in your writing varies the words you use. That will make your writing more interesting and engaging to readers.

Extra

Look at a newspaper. Headlines sometimes use words that have synonyms in the stories. See if you can find a pair of headline/story synonyms.

Grammar Connection

Words with opposite meanings are called *antonyms*.

Pre-Activity

Play a game with some friends. Take turns saying a word. The first person to say the opposite of that word gets a point. The first one to get ten points wins.

Activity

A. Read the paragraph.

In a time when women were not encouraged to fly, Amelia Earhart had dreams that soared. In the 1920s, the young Earhart took flying lessons. Aviation was a <u>dangerous</u> and <u>unknown</u> field then— even for men! But that didn't stop Earhart from purchasing her own plane. In 1932, Earhart made aviation history by becoming the first woman to fly alone across the Atlantic Ocean. After she <u>finished</u> that safe trip, Earhart continued to set records in speed and distance. But it's her <u>last</u> trip that is her most famous. In 1937, she set out to fly around the world. More than a month after she started this trip, Earhart's plane disappeared over the Pacific Ocean. A huge search found no trace of the famous pilot. Historians are <u>unsure</u> about what happened to Earhart. But one thing is certain: She left a substantial mark on aviation history.

B. Look at the underlined words in the paragraph. An antonym for each one can be found in the paragraph. Write each pair you find.

unknown   *famous*

_____ _____

_____ _____

_____ _____

_____ _____

Extra

Find some information about Earhart's disappearance. What do you think happened?

Post-Activity

Work with a partner. Choose a magazine article and both read it. Then each of you should list ten words from the article. Trade lists. Then try to find antonyms and synonyms for the words on the lists.

Pre-Activity

Did you ever give a speech? You have probably heard someone give a speech. Did the speaker try to persuade, or convince, the listeners about something—perhaps to vote or to give money to a good cause? Did the speaker succeed or fail?

Activity

A. *Succeed* and *fail* are opposites. Unscramble the letters to find an antonym for each word below.

1. slow
   CIUKQ _____

2. give
   KATE _____

3. full
   METYP _____

4. exciting
   DLUL _____

5. brave
   RAAIDF _____

6. worst
   TESB _____

7. lie
   RUTHT _____

8. still
   VEATIC _____

9. least
   SOTM _____

10. nervous
    ALCM _____

B. Use some of the unscrambled words to complete these sentences.

1. Before speaking in front of an audience, don't forget to

   _____ a deep breath.

2. This will help you feel _____.

3. To make sure their speech isn't _____, some

   of the best speakers begin with a joke.

4. To tell the _____, almost everyone

   is _____ to give a speech.

5. The _____ advice about making
   a speech is to practice.

Writing Tip

Writing that tries to influence behavior or convince people to take action is called *persuasive* writing. Persuasive writing, like a speech, requires careful planning ahead. Making a list is a good way to plan what you want to say in your writing. Remember, words that have opposite meanings are *antonyms*.

C. Pretend you are a candidate for Food Selector. If elected, you get to choose all the food that the school cafeteria serves. What a great job! You have to give a campaign speech to let the students know why they should elect you. Before you start writing your speech, think about some of your plans for the job. What are your qualifications? Make a list of points you want to make in your speech.

Brainstorming List: _____

_____

_____

_____

Now, write your speech. Try to include some of the words from Activity A.

_____

_____

_____

_____

_____

_____

_____

_____

_____

_____

_____

_____

Extra

If you heard someone you didn't like give a great speech, might you begin to like that person more? Why or why not?

Post-Activity

Practice your speech. Then read it out loud to some family members. Ask them if they would vote for you.

Pre-Activity

There is going to be a new playground.
They're taking a poll to find out what children want.
My favorite thing to do is to climb and slide down the pole
of the jungle gym. What's yours, Jim?

Which pairs of words in the sentences sound alike?
Try to think of some other pairs of words that sound alike.

Activity

A. Underline the words that sound alike.

1. The teacher allowed the students to read aloud.

2. Although deer eat her flowers, my dear Aunt Sally still enjoys seeing them.

3. The custodian in the pale blue shirt emptied her pail.

4. Kevin's role in the play involves eating a roll at a diner.

5. Jasmine, please come here so you can hear me.

B. Circle the correct word to complete each sentence.

1. Did you eat the (pear, pair) I left for you on the table?

2. Please (right, write) a letter to your grandfather and I will mail it for you.

3. May I please have a (peace, piece) of the pie?

4. The department store downtown is having a huge (sale, sail) on fishing rods.

5. Whenever Wanda throws a party, she always has far (to, two, too) much food.

Post-Activity

Work with a friend. Each pick a page from a favorite book. Then count the number of homonyms you find on that page. See who found the most.

Grammar Connection

Homonyms are words that sound the same but have different spellings and meanings.

Extra

The words *to*, *too*, and *two* are a homonym threesome. Can you think of another set of homonyms that come in three? Hint: A common set begins with the letters *th*.

Language Strategy

When a homonym is used in speech, the careful listener can tell which word is meant by the way it is used in the sentence.

Extra

Homonyms are everywhere! Read the instructions for the Pre-Activity again. How many words have homonyms?

Pre-Activity

Play a trick. Say these words aloud and ask a friend to write them on a piece of paper:

plain   bear

Look at what your friend wrote. Did he or she write homonyms for the words? (plane, bare) If so, tell him or her that the words are spelled wrong. See how long before your friend catches on to what you're doing.

Activity

A. Complete each sentence with the correct word.

sent   cent   scent

1. Charles's mother _____ him to the store to get flour and salt.

2. Later, a wonderful _____ drifted from the kitchen.

3. His grandmother said that when she was a girl, a pretzel stick cost one _____.

B. Each group of letters can be rearranged to spell a homonym of the word paired with it. Unscramble each word and write the pair of homonyms on the lines.

1. HINTG _*night*_
   GIKTHN _*knight*_

2. ATEM _____
   TEME _____

3. ONW _____
   EON _____

4. RTEWI _____
   TGHIR _____

5. LAINP _____
   LEAPN _____

6. IFRA _____
   RAFE _____

7. LUFOR _____
   WORELF _____

8. DAER _____
   DRE _____

Post-Activity

Writing a sentence that uses two homonyms is not easy. Try writing a couple in your journal.

Pre-Activity

Have you ever heard someone say it's "raining cats and dogs"? Does that mean cats and dogs are falling from the sky? Is it good or bad when someone says, "You're the apple of my eye"? Do you know any other expressions like these?

Activity

A. Each sentence below contains an idiom that is underlined. Write what you think each one means.

1. Greta put her <u>John Hancock</u> on the contract.

   _____

2. Since Linda left her new baseball mitt out in the rain, she's been <u>in the doghouse</u>.

   _____

3. My sister loves studying algebra, but it is <u>Greek to me</u>.

   _____

4. Good answer! You <u>hit the nail on the head</u>.

   _____

5. Before school starts, you better <u>turn over a new leaf</u>.

   _____

B. Match each idiom to its meaning.

1. John Hancock   change

2. in the doghouse   exactly right

3. Greek to me   in trouble

4. hit the nail on the head   signature

5. turn over a new leaf   difficult

Post-Activity

Use an idiom at lunch or dinner. Do people know what you mean? Ask them about others they may know. Later, list some idioms in your journal.

Grammar Connection

An *idiom* is a group of words that when used together mean something different from what those same words mean when used on their own.

Extra

For fun, make up your own idiom. Choose one that makes sense and that you can explain. Then start to use it. See if other people start using it, too.

Grammar Connection

A *prefix* is a group of letters added to the front of a word that gives the word a different meaning.

Pre-Activity

The teacher wanted to preview the film before the class could view it. Then he wanted students to review it. The words *preview* and *review* are based on the word *view*. Can you figure out what *pre* and *re* mean?

Activity

A. Add one of these prefixes to each word to create a new word. Then match to the definition.

| re   un   dis   in |

1. *re*store   a. hidden or unseen

2. _____appear   b. because of bad luck

3. _____fortunately   c. put back

4. _____visible   d. to be out of sight

B. Fill in each blank with a word you created above.

The Great Smoky Mountains National Park is visited more than any other U.S. park. _____, the park is having trouble with air pollution and acid rain. Scientists are trying to stop the pollution and _____ clean air. The pollution is not how the mountains got their name. The name comes from a natural blue mist that floats in the mountains. The mist is made up of tiny, nearly _____ drops of water vapor and plant oil from the park's millions of trees. Some mountaintops seem to _____ into the clouds.

Post-Activity

Have you ever been to the Great Smoky Mountains or another park? Write about the experience in your journal. Or write about an imaginary trip to the top of a mountain. Then look at the sentences you wrote. Circle any prefixes you used.

23

Pre-Activity

Adding a prefix to a word changes that word's meaning. Sometimes it changes a word to its opposite. What prefix would change these two words to their opposites?

popular   true

Activity

A. Create new—and opposite—words by adding one of these prefixes. Each of these prefixes means "not."

un	im	in

1. _im_ + possible = ___impossible___

2. ____ + active = _____

3. ____ + known = _____

4. ____ + proper = _____

5. ____ + correct = _____

B. Use one of the words above and its antonym to complete each sentence.

1. Most people think it is _____ to become

   president, but I think anything is _____.

2. Rosa was happy because she had nine _____

   answers and only one _____ answer.

3. Many animals, such as bats, are _____ at

   night and _____ during the day.

4. Almost overnight he went from being a penniless,

   _____ writer to being a _____ celebrity.

5. Clay thinks wearing a hat at the table is _____

   behavior, but his mom says it is highly _____.

Post-Activity

Try to think of three prefixes that are not on this page. Make a list of five words for each one. (You may want to use a dictionary.)

Language Strategy

Knowing what a prefix means is a great way to add dozens of words to your vocabulary.

Extra

Do all words that begin with *un* or *in* mean "no"? Can you think of an example or two?

Grammar Connection

A *suffix* is a group of letters added to the end of a word that changes the word's meaning. Often the suffix changes the word's part of speech, too.

Extra

Sometimes when you add a suffix to a word, the spelling of the original word must change slightly.

For example:
pretty + est = prettiest
dance + ing = dancing
believe + able = believable
Can you think of a few more words like this?

Pre-Activity

Think of a verb, such as *walk, travel,* or *teach.* Now think of that word with an *er* on the end. What part of speech is your new word? What happens to *kind* when you add *ness* to it? Can you think of other groups of letters that change words?

Activity

A. Here are some common suffixes. Add a word of your own to form a new word.

1. _____ed   6. _____ness

2. _____er   7. _____less

3. _____ing   8. _____ship

4. _____ment   9. _____ion

5. _____ly   10. _____able

B. The word that you add the suffix to is called the *root word.* Each of the words below has a suffix. Write the root word for each.

1. enjoyable   _enjoy_   7. vastly   _____

2. injection   _____   8. renewable _____

3. friendship _____   9. properly   _____

4. walking   _____   10. goodness _____

5. publisher   _____   11. emotional _____

6. parked   _____   12. greatest _____

Post-Activity

In your journal, write a few sentences about a current news event from the past week. Then go back and circle any suffixes you used.

Pre-Activity

What are some words that might describe grass? For example, grass that is very green and well cared for might be described as *velvety*. Imagine what velvet feels like.

Activity

A. Pretend you see two lawns. One is like a golf course and the other looks as if no one has cared for it in years. Choose four adjectives to describe each lawn.

| tidy | manicured | abandoned | neglected |
| yellowed | lush | dried-out | flourishing |

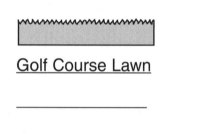

Golf Course Lawn

_____

_____

_____

_____

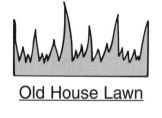

Old House Lawn

_____

_____

_____

_____

B. Now imagine that you have been hired to take care of the abandoned lawn. Describe what you would do. Use some of the adjectives from above. You might also use some of these verbs.

| fertilize | mow | trim | water | plant |

_____

_____

_____

_____

_____

Post-Activity

Show your paragraph to a family member. Would he or she hire you?

Grammar Connection

Adjectives describe and/or tell about a noun or pronoun. Adjectives answer the following questions: *what kind?* *how many?* *what one?*

Extra

If you have a lawn at home, ask if you can help take care of it. If not, can you volunteer to help at a local park, church, or community center?

Language Strategy

Adjectives are powerful words. They tell us more information and help us make important decisions. Color words, like *red* and *purple*, are adjectives. So are numbers: *one purple* grape, *two red* monkeys.

Extra

Think about the power of the words *pretty* and *ugly*.

Pre-Activity

If someone told you he or she had a cookie to give away, you'd probably want it, right? But if he or she told you it's a *stale* cookie, would you change your mind? What adjective would "change your opinion" of the word *cat*? How about a *roller coaster*?

Activity

A. For each word, write two adjectives that might describe it. Try to use adjectives that are very different from each other.

1. elephant _____

2. kangaroo _____

3. path _____

4. tree _____

5. eagle _____

6. weather _____

7. snacks _____

8. aquarium _____

9. penguin _____

B. Choose a noun from Activity A. Use it along with your adjectives in a sentence.

_____

_____

_____

_____

_____

Post-Activity

In your journal, write a pretend e-mail to your cousin about a class field trip to the zoo. Try to use at least five adjectives.

Pre-Activity

An old saying goes "a picture is worth a thousand words." Look at a picture in your classroom. Think of some words that describe it. Then ask someone else to describe it. Do your words agree?

Activity

Imagine what this young man might do to deserve to have his picture in the newspaper. Use these adjectives and some of your own to write an article about him.

| outstanding prestigious remarkable brave |
| heroic modest sunny proud smart |

_____

_____

_____

_____

_____

_____

_____

_____

_____

_____

Post-Activity

Select a picture from a newspaper and show it—but not the article—to a family member. Then try to guess what the story is about. Together, read the article.

Writing Tip

Adjectives help paint a clearer picture for the listener or reader. Using adjectives in your writing makes it more vivid and precise.

Extra

Ask a family member to look through some old family photos with you. Together think of at least one adjective to describe each picture.

Grammar Connection

An *adverb* modifies or describes a verb, an adjective, or another adverb. Adverbs tell:
how
when
where
how often
to what extent

Extra

Watch the weather on the local television news. Listen for adverbs.

Pre-Activity

On a dry, sunny day, some people might drive fast. But in a wintry snowstorm, they probably will drive slowly or more cautiously. *Fast, slowly, more,* and *cautiously* describe how the person drives. Can you think of another word to describe how a person might drive?

Activity

A. Choose the adverb that you think best describes each verb.

1. rain sprinkles   a. swiftly
2. thunder roars   b. brightly
3. snowflakes fall   c. loudly
4. sun shines   d. gently
5. temperature rose   e. quietly
6. raging river flows   f. steadily

B. Choose one of the matches you made above and draw a picture of it. Write two adverbs to describe what is happening in the picture.

Post-Activity

Keep a weather journal for a week. Each morning write your predictions for the day's weather. Use as many adverbs as you can. Each evening, record what happened that day. How accurate were your weather predictions?

Pre-Activity

Read these sentences.

Harlan answered the question.

Harlan answered the question quickly and correctly.

The words *quickly* and *correctly* tell us when and how Harlan answered. They give us information that is clearer and more exact. Think of three more words that could describe ways a question can be answered.

Activity

A. Use these adverbs to make the story clearer.

| immediately | beautifully | always |
| brightly | loudly | excitedly |

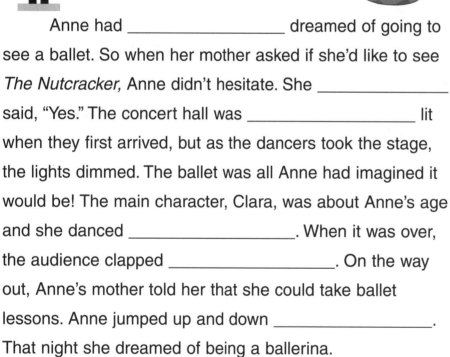

Anne had _____ dreamed of going to see a ballet. So when her mother asked if she'd like to see *The Nutcracker,* Anne didn't hesitate. She _____ said, "Yes." The concert hall was _____ lit when they first arrived, but as the dancers took the stage, the lights dimmed. The ballet was all Anne had imagined it would be! The main character, Clara, was about Anne's age and she danced _____. When it was over, the audience clapped _____. On the way out, Anne's mother told her that she could take ballet lessons. Anne jumped up and down _____. That night she dreamed of being a ballerina.

B. Use the adverbs *happily* and *everywhere* in a
    sentence. _____

_____

Post-Activity

At lunch or dinner, use some adverbs to describe the cooking. Are the vegetables cooked *perfectly*? Is the dessert baked *exceptionally*? Be sure to tell the chef!

Writing Tip

Adverbs help us to be more specific in our speech and writing.

Not only do they tell how, when, and where, they tell to what extent.
A cake can be good or *really* good.

Adverbs can also be used to compare actions.

Gunther leaps high when he dances, but Bethany leaps *higher*.

Extra

What kind of lessons would you like to take? Think of some adverbs and adjectives that you could use to describe the lessons.

Grammar Connection

A *sentence* should express a complete thought. A *sentence* contains a *subject* (noun or pronoun) and a *predicate* (verb).

There are four types of sentences:

Interrogative (a question): Where are you going?

Declarative (a statement): I am going to Timbuktu.

Exclamatory (exclamation): Why, that is wonderful!

Imperative (a command): Take me.

Pre-Activity

The dog barked.
The dog barked loudly.
Otto barked.
Otto loud

Which of the above is *not* a sentence? Think of a sentence about a dog you know.

Activity

A. There are four types of sentences: interrogative, declarative, exclamatory, and imperative. Each sentence below is one of these types. Label each one.

1. What did you say? _____

2. I told the dog to come here. _____

3. He ran the other way. _____

4. I can't believe he did that! _____

5. That's too bad. _____

6. I'll get a treat. _____

7. Come, Duke, come. _____

8. Now that's a good dog! _____

B. Write a sentence of each type. Try writing about a cat or your favorite kind of wild animal.

_____

_____

_____

_____

_____

_____

Post-Activity

Do you know what a *fragment* is? Make up a couple of examples of fragments about a pet. Challenge a friend to turn your fragments into sentences.

Pre-Activity

Close your eyes and think about the word *food*. What images do you see? Pizza? Cake? Salad? The neat thing about most words is they make you think of other words. What words come to mind when you see the word *restaurant*? How about *picnic*?

Activity

A. Think about these food words and place them into the best category.

hamburger	eggs	carrot sticks	waffles
pork chops	candy	orange juice	potato
chicken	pretzels	potato chips	cereal

<u>Snacks</u>   <u>Breakfast</u>   <u>Dinner</u>

_____   _____   _____

_____   _____   _____

_____   _____   _____

_____   _____   _____

B. Now think of at least four words for each of these categories. You might want to consult a cookbook.

1. Ways to cook eggs:

_____

2. Desserts:

_____

3. Cooking equipment:

_____

Language Strategy

Using word associations or thinking about words in groups or categories can really expand vocabulary and improve writing.

COOKBOOK

C. Pretend you have been asked to write a cookbook for beginners. Choose one of the categories and words on page 32 and write the opening to that chapter. Let your imagination sizzle.

THE GOOD COOKBOOK

Written and Illustrated by _____

_____

_____

_____

_____

_____

_____

_____

_____

_____

_____

_____

_____

_____

_____

_____

Extra

Choose a recipe and ask an adult family member to help you cook it. If it turns out well, make it again as a gift for a friend.

Post-Activity

The next time you are in the library or a bookstore, find the cookbook section. Can you believe there are so many different kinds! In your journal, list some of the titles. Copy a recipe that you might want to try.

Pre-Activity

What words do you think of when you hear bees?
You probably thought of the words *buzz* and *sting*.
But what about *busy* and *hive* and *swarm*? If you
have ever seen a beehive, tell someone about it.

Activity

A. Read this poem about bees by Linda Oatman High.

A swarm in May
is worth a load of hay.
A swarm in June
is a silver spoon.
A swarm in July
isn't worth a fly.

Answer these questions about the poem.

1. Do you think that "worth a load of hay" is a good thing?
   Why or why not?

   _____

   _____

2. What words in the poem let you know that a swarm of
   bees in June make a lot of honey?

   _____

   _____

3. Do you think that bees in July make as much honey as
   bees in May and June? Why or why not?

   _____

   _____

B. On another sheet of paper, write your own poem
about bees. Use some of these "bee" words.

honey	hive	honeycomb
swarm	beekeeper	buzz

Post-Activity

Read your poem to a family member. Write a few
sentences about the experience in your journal.

Language Strategy

Careful reading is
important. Sometimes
authors don't speak in a
straightforward manner.
Instead, the reader has to
figure out the meaning.

Extra

Honey comes in many
varieties, depending on
the type of flower the
bees visited. Clover
honey is one of the most
common types. Ask a
family member to
purchase two different
types of honey. Then do a
taste-test comparison.

Grammar Connection

Words can help us describe how we feel in different situations. Words that describe how we feel are usually *adjectives*. In fact, they are often special kinds of adjectives called *predicate adjectives*.

Extra

Do you know the expression "at a loss for words"? Can you think of a time when you felt at a loss for words?

Pre-Activity

Have you ever seen a movie that made you cry? You were probably sad during that movie. *Sad* describes your feelings. How would you feel if you saw a movie that made you laugh? How about if you saw a horror movie?

Activity

A. Circle the word that best describes how you might feel if you . . .

1. . . . saw a large hairy spider on your bed?
   a. terrific   b. horrified   c. calm

2. . . . looked up and saw a boulder headed toward you?
   a. terrified   b. silly   c. happy

3. . . . learned that you got an A on a test you thought you were not prepared for?
   a. relieved   b. sad   c. sleepy

4. . . . won a contest?
   a. awful   b. overjoyed   c. confused

B. How do you think most people feel when they see a small hurt puppy or kitten? Write about it here. Use some of these words along with your own.

> tender   maternal   kindly   loving   helpless
> helpful   caring   nurturing   worried

_____

_____

_____

_____

_____

_____

Post-Activity

Think about the last time someone praised your work. Make a list of words that describe how that made you feel. Tell the words to that person. You'll probably make her or him feel happy!

Pre-Activity

Words can have more than one association. What do you think of when you hear the word *hot*—temperature or spicy food? How about the word *cold*? Do you need a tissue or a jacket?

Not only does the word *desert* have two meanings, there are two ways to pronounce it. One is de-sert´ (dĭ•zûrt´) and the other is des´-ert (dĕź•ərt). Read the sentence below out loud.

Did the soldier desert his troop in the desert?

Activity

Circle the words that make sense in this article about a hot, dry desert.

Deserts get very little rainfall. It takes special kinds of animals and plants to survive in such a harsh climate. But many do. The (dolphin, camel) can go for a long time without drinking water. For this reason, (Bedouin, Eskimo) people ride them as they make their way through the desert. If you are looking for water in a desert, you might be happy to find a (maple tree, cactus). This fleshy desert plant holds water. If you're lucky enough to find an (ocean, oasis) in the desert, you'll probably find water there, too.

Post-Activity

Look at a globe or an atlas and make a list of some of the biggest deserts in the world. Pick one and find some information about it online or in a library. In your journal, write the three most interesting facts you find.

Writing Tip

You may already be familiar with the concept of *cause and effect* from your study of math and science. Something happens that leads to a particular result. Good writers use cause-and-effect concepts, too.

"Clue words" help identify cause-and-effect sentences. Some of these words are *so, because,* and *if.*

Extra

Can you think of a movie you've seen that used cause-and-effect in its plot?

Pre-Activity

Because they forecasted snow, I wore my boots.

Shannon went to bed at 8:00 because she has to get up early tomorrow.

I needed peace and quiet, so I went into my room.

These sentences show *cause and effect*. For example, "Because they forecasted snow" is the *cause*. "I wore my boots" is the *effect*. Work with a friend and identify the cause and effect in the other sentences.

Activity

Each of these sentences is missing either the cause or the effect. Read each carefully and look for clue words. Then fill in the blanks with a logical cause or effect. The first one is done for you.

1. Because we let our dog out in the rain, *he got water all over the carpet when he came inside.*

2. Because the man's tie was too tight, _____ _____.

3. If you are good tonight, _____ _____.

4. _____, so that all the kids in my class could have a cookie.

5. Because you answered the question correctly, _____ _____.

Post-Activity

Now have some fun writing in your journal. Complete each sentence above with an illogical, silly answer. For example, Because we let our dog out in the rain, <u>he took a taxi to Palm Beach</u>.

37

Pre-Activity

Do you like to read about faraway lands or strange animals? Or are you interested in cars, sports, or art? Reading helps us learn about new topics. Tell a friend an unusual fact you learned from reading.

Activity

A. Read and then answer the questions below.

Chameleons, Arctic foxes, and snowshoe hares are some animals that use camouflage to try to blend into their environment. Changing the color of their skin or fur protects them from hunters and other animals. In the winter, the white fur of the Arctic fox and the snowshoe hare blends with the snow, making them more difficult to see.

A chameleon's skin can change as it moves, and it can take less than a minute. The changes involve many different colors that the lizards use to disguise themselves in a wide variety of surroundings.

1. In the first sentence, what two words give you an idea of

   the meaning of *camouflage*? _____

   _____

2. In the second sentence, what word tells you what changing the color of fur and skin can do for an animal?

   _____

3. In sentence three, what two animals are the same color?

   _____

4. In the last sentence, what word is a synonym for

   camouflage? _____

B. You can "apply what you learn." Why do you think a polar bear is white?

   _____

   _____

   _____

Language Strategy

Reading for meaning helps improve our knowledge and our skills with language. Always check what you write to make sure you have provided enough information.

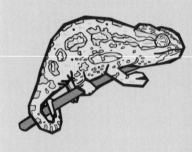

C. What kind of uniform does a soldier wear in the jungle? Draw a picture here and then write about how the uniform helped save the soldier's life.

_____

_____

_____

_____

_____

_____

_____

_____

_____

_____

_____

_____

_____

_____

_____

_____

_____

Extra

Sometimes a person might be described as a *chameleon*. What do you think this says about that person?

Post-Activity

Work with a partner. Read your partner a short article from a magazine. Then ask three questions about it. Is he or she able to answer correctly? Now have your partner do the same for you. Remember to listen carefully!

Pre-Activity

Can you name a famous inventor? The world would be quite a different place without inventors like Alexander Graham Bell and Thomas Edison. Do you know what each of these inventors is most famous for?

Activity

A. Circle the pictures of the things we would not be able to use if we did not have electricity.

B. Write a story about living in a time before electricity. Think about how you would see at night. How would you cook dinner or keep warm?

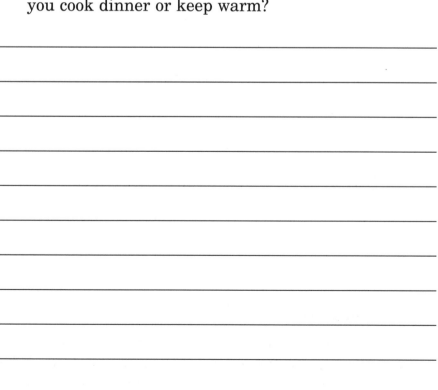

Writing Tip

Writing so that people can picture an object or a place takes careful thought and choice of words. Remember, words that describe are *adjectives* and *adverbs*.

Before you start writing anything, it's a wise idea to spend some time thinking through the idea and/or researching it. Making a list of good descriptive words will help, too.

C. Circle the word that best completes each sentence.

Benjamin Franklin lived at a time before electricity. He read and wrote by candlelight. However, Franklin was a person of great (fatigue   foresight). He was one of the first people to experiment with electricity. Franklin lived and (conducted   abducted) his work in Philadelphia. In one of his experiments, he flew a homemade kite during a thunderstorm and proved that lightning is electricity. He (harnessed   tamed) lightning by using a lightning rod. What Franklin did was (diligent   dangerous), but it laid the groundwork for many of the things we use today.

D. Think of something unusual that you would like to have—maybe a personal robot, a flying car, or an invisible pet. Imagine that you have invented the device. Now write an article for a newspaper describing the invention.

_____

_____

_____

_____

_____

_____

_____

_____

_____

Extra

New devices are invented nearly every day. Can you think of one or two items that have been invented in your lifetime?

Post-Activity

Read your article to a friend or family member. Ask if he or she can picture your invention. Write some of your best descriptive words in your journal.

Pre-Activity

Try to remember a time when you wanted your parents to do something special for you. What did you do or say to get them to agree with you? Are there some special words you used? Did you tell them all the good things about it? Did you finally persuade them? Share this experience with a friend.

Activity

Think about what you "invented" in the previous lesson. You already wrote an article describing your invention. Now you need to write an article or design an ad that will convince people to purchase your invention.

A. First make a list of words you will use.

_____   _____   _____

_____   _____   _____

_____   _____   _____

B. Write the article or show the ad here. Remember, you want to persuade people to try your invention.

Writing Tip

Remember, writing that tries to influence behavior or convince people to take action is called *persuasive* writing. Words such as these are often used in persuasive writing: *please, consider, remember, benefit, results,* and *saving.* People who develop advertisements must be good persuasive writers.

Extra

What is your favorite ad? Why?

Post-Activity

Show your article or ad to a friend. Would he or she purchase your invention? Why or why not? Do you need to make some changes?

Writing Tip

There are many kinds of books and articles. An author who writes a lot about one topic is a specialty writer. For example, there are sports journalists, travel writers, movie reviewers, and cookbook authors. But no matter what the specialty, all need to have strong language skills.

Extra

It's never too early to start exploring your creative interests! Take some time tomorrow to paint, write, draw, act, or do whatever creative activity that interests you.

Pre-Activity

Has anyone ever told you that you are creative? Maybe you like to draw, dance, or make up funny stories. Many jobs allow people to be creative. Some people design book covers, others create sculpture, some write plays. Do you know anyone who has a "creative" job?

Activity

Pretend you work for a magazine. Your editor wants you to write an article about the work of a creative person. You can choose a real person or create one of your own. Use words from the word bank and some of your own.

inventive	artistic	imagination
compose	satisfying	original

Creative Work Is Fun!

An article by _____

_____

_____

_____

_____

_____

_____

_____

_____

_____

_____

_____

Post-Activity

Think of three creative jobs that you might like to have someday. List them in your journal. Then talk with a family member about the merits of each job.

Pre-Activity

Have you ever tried to solve a problem by talking it out with a friend? Or have you and your classmates ever tried to come up with a surprise for your teacher? You probably had lots and lots of ideas and then picked one.

With a friend, think of some things that would help make the world a better place. Write down every idea that comes to mind.

Activity

Choose one of your ideas to "flesh out."

1. Describe your idea here. _____
_____
_____
_____

2. Write two things that would help you realize this idea, such as education and planning.
_____
_____

3. List two or more obstacles that might get in the way of your dream, such as money and not enough time.
_____
_____
_____

4. For each hardship you listed in question 3, list some ways to overcome it.
_____
_____
_____

Post-Activity

Write this idea in your journal and put today's date by it. As you think of other dreams, goals, or ambitions, write those down and date them, too. You'll have a fascinating record to look back on someday!

Writing Tip

Brainstorming is a very useful tool for a writer. When you brainstorm, you think of all possible solutions to a problem or ideas about a topic. You write each one down, no matter how "far out" it might seem. When you "rev up" your brain, you'll be surprised by how many great ideas pop out.

Extra

Talk about your dreams and ambitions. Ask an adult to tell you some of the dreams he or she had at your age. Did they come true?

Writing Tip

Good writers are good readers, so read a lot. Remember to think for a bit before you start writing. You might even want to make a list of some of the things you want to write about in your story.

Pre-Activity

Think about reading just for fun. Do you like to read a mystery book and finally learn "who done it?" Or do you like an adventure story? Many authors say that the process of *writing* a story is as much fun as reading one.

Activity

Have fun writing a story. You can use one of these two ideas or choose one of your own. If you run out of room here, continue on another piece of paper.

Theme 1:
Write about a girl who loves baseball so much that she tries out for the school's all-boy baseball team and makes it. Are the other players nice to her? Does she enjoy playing it as much as watching? What happens on the day of the big game?

Theme 2:
Write about a house cat who accidentally gets locked outside. She wanders too far from home and can't find her way back. What happens when a giant rainstorm hits? How does she find her way back? What happens when she gets back in the house?

_____

_____

_____

_____

_____

_____

_____

_____

Post-Activity

Get together with a friend and each suggest a book for the other to read. After you've read the books, talk about them. Did your friend like your book as much as you did?

Pre-Activity

Writing is everywhere, not just in books and magazines. Good writing and communication skills are necessary to do practically anything. As you go through your day's routine, notice each time you speak, write, or read something.

Activity

One way people communicate is by writing letters. Sometimes letters work better than talking on the phone or sending an e-mail. Writing a letter gives you more time to choose your words carefully. A letter should include these five parts:

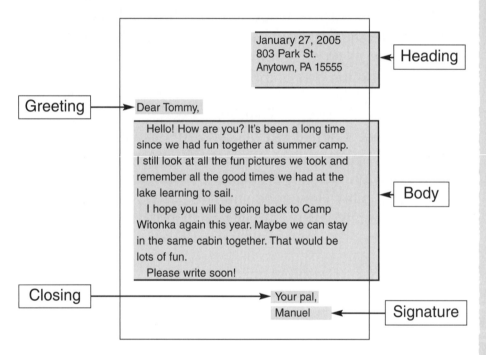

Pick a person you would like to write a letter to. It can be a person you know, like a friend or relative. Or it could be someone you admire, like a celebrity or an author. It could even be someone from long ago whom you like reading about, such as Abraham Lincoln or Martin Luther King, Jr. What would you want to say to this person? Here's your chance. On another sheet of paper, write your letter!

Post-Activity

Review your letter. Did you use correct spelling? If you're not sure, check a dictionary. Also, make sure you used proper grammar and punctuation. A good writer always double-checks.

46

ANSWER KEY

Page 5
A. 1. b 2. e 3. a 4. c 5. d

B. Students should circle *peel, core,* and *slice.*

C. Sentences will vary.

Pages 6–7
A. 1. b 2. d 3. a 4. c

B. The following words should be underlined:
   1. drop 2. grow 3. sprout 4. thrive

C. Stories will vary.

D. Drawings will vary.

Page 8
A. Word lists will vary.

B. The following words should be circled:
   1. live 2. flying 3. eat 4. scream

Page 9
Folktales will vary.

Pages 10–11
A. Students should draw lines to match the following:
   1. camel - desert
   2. monkey - jungle
   3. whale - ocean
   4. cow - pasture
   5. bear - cave
   6. crocodile - swamp

B.

Animal	Habitat
iguana	desert
horse	pasture
bat	cave
shark	ocean
alligator	swamp
elephant	jungle

C. Answers will vary.

D. Paragraphs will vary.

Page 12
A. 1. b 2. d 3. a 4. e 5. c

B. Answers will vary.

Page 13
A.

Cities	Countries	Oceans
Toronto	Mexico	Indian
Seattle	Argentina	Atlantic
London	U.S.A.	Arctic
San Francisco	China	Pacific
Tokyo	France	Antarctic

B. Answers will vary.

Page 14
A. 1. Just finishing the race was a big accomplishment for Ramal.
   2. Shan seems to have natural athletic ability.
   3. It took great courage to say no to the man's offer.
   4. Anne needs permission from her parents to enter the contest.
   5. Ellen's friendliness made the girls feel welcome.

B. Sentences will vary.

Page 15
A. Students should draw lines to match the following:
   1. career - j. profession
   2. artist - d. illustrator
   3. teacher - h. educator
   4. athlete - c. sportsman
   5. accountant - g. bookkeeper
   6. actor - a. performer
   7. carpenter - e. builder
   8. lawyer - b. attorney
   9. writer - f. author
   10. chef - i. cook

B. Answers will vary.

Page 16
1. happiness - joy
2. car - automobile
3. united - together
4. poor - penniless
5. wet - soaked
6. nightfall - dusk
7. quiet - silent
8. tune - melody
9. give - donate
10. glow - shine
11. get - obtain
12. crash - collision
13. sadness - sorrow
14. violin - fiddle

Page 17
B.

dangerous	famous
unknown	safe
finished	started
last	first
unsure	certain

Pages 18–19
A. 1. slow - quick   6. worst - best
   2. give - take   7. lie - truth
   3. full - empty   8. still - active
   4. exciting - dull 9. least - most
   5. brave - afraid 10. nervous - calm

B. 1. Before speaking in front of an audience, don't forget to take a deep breath.
   2. This will help you feel calm.
   3. To make sure their speech isn't dull, some of the best speakers begin with a joke.
   4. To tell the truth, almost everyone is afraid to give a speech.
   5. The best advice about making a speech is to practice.

C. Lists and speeches will vary.

Page 20
A. 1. The teacher allowed the students to read aloud.
   2. Although deer eat her flowers, my dear Aunt Sally still enjoys seeing them.
   3. The custodian in the pale blue shirt emptied her pail.
   4. Kevin's role in the play involves eating a roll at a diner.
   5. Jasmine, please come here so you can hear me.

B. 1. Did you eat the (pear) I left for you on the table?
   2. Please (write) a letter to your grandfather and I will mail it for you.
   3. May I please have a (piece) of the pie?
   4. The department store downtown is having a huge (sale) on fishing rods.
   5. Whenever Wanda throws a party, she always has far (too) much food.

Page 21
A. 1. Charles's mother sent him to the store to get flour and salt.
   2. Later, a wonderful scent drifted from the kitchen.
   3. His grandmother said that when she was a girl, a pretzel stick cost one cent.

B. 1. night   5. plain
      knight   plane
   2. meat   6. fair
      meet   fare
   3. won   7. flour
      one   flower
   4. write   8. read
      right   red

Page 22
A. 1. signature
   2. in trouble
   3. doesn't make sense; is too hard
   4. exactly right
   5. make a new start; change

B. Students should draw lines to match the following:
   1. John Hancock - signature
   2. in the doghouse - in trouble
   3. Greek to me - difficult
   4. hit the nail on the head - exactly right
   5. turn over a new leaf - change

Page 23
A. Students should draw lines to match the following:
   1. restore - c. put back
   2. disappear - a. hidden or unseen
   3. unfortunately - b. because of bad luck
   4. invisible - d. to be out of sight

B. The Great Smoky Mountains National Park is visited more than any other U.S. park. Unfortunately, the park is having trouble with air pollution and acid rain. Scientists are trying to stop the pollution and restore clean air. The pollution is not how the mountains got their name. The name comes from a natural blue mist that floats in the mountains. The mist is made up of tiny, nearly invisible drops of water vapor and plant oil from the park's millions of trees. Some mountaintops seem to disappear into the clouds.

Page 24
A. 1. impossible   4. improper
   2. inactive   5. incorrect
   3. unknown

B. 1. Most people think it is <u>impossible</u> to
     become president, but I think anything is
     <u>possible</u>.
   2. Rosa was happy because she had nine
     <u>correct</u> answers and only one <u>incorrect</u>
     answer.
   3. Many animals, such as bats, are <u>active</u>
     at night and <u>inactive</u> during the day.
   4. Almost overnight he went from being a
     penniless, <u>unknown</u> writer to being a
     <u>known</u> celebrity.
   5. Clay thinks wearing a hat at the table is
     <u>proper</u> behavior, but his mom says it is
     highly <u>improper</u>.

Page 25
A. Answers will vary.

B. 1. enjoy   7. vast
   2. inject   8. renew
   3. friend   9. proper
   4. walk   10. good
   5. publish   11. emotion
   6. park   12. great

Page 26
A. <u>Golf Course Lawn</u>   <u>Old House Lawn</u>
   tidy   abandoned
   lush   neglected
   manicured   yellowed
   flourishing   dried-out

B. Answers will vary.

Page 27
A. Answers will vary.

B. Answers will vary.

Page 28
Articles will vary.

Page 29
A. Students should draw lines to match the
   following:
   1. rain sprinkles gently
   2. thunder roars loudly
   3. snowflakes fall quietly
   4. sun shines brightly
   5. temperature rose steadily
   6. raging river flows swiftly

B. Drawings and adverbs will vary.

Page 30
   Anne had <u>always</u> dreamed of going to see a
ballet. So when her mother asked if she'd like
to see *The Nutcracker,* Anne didn't hesitate.
She <u>immediately</u> said, "Yes." The concert hall
was <u>brightly</u> lit when they first arrived, but as
the dancers took the stage, the lights dimmed.
The ballet was all Anne had imagined it would
be! The main character, Clara, was about
Anne's age and she danced <u>beautifully</u>. When
it was over, the audience clapped <u>loudly</u>. On
the way out, Anne's mother told her that she
could take ballet lessons. Anne jumped up
and down <u>excitedly</u>. That night she dreamed
of being a ballerina.

Page 31
A. 1. interrogative
   2. declarative
   3. declarative
   4. exclamatory
   5. declarative
   6. declarative
   7. imperative
   8. exclamatory

B. Sentences will vary.

Pages 32–33
A. <u>Snacks</u>   <u>Breakfast</u>   <u>Dinner</u>
   carrot sticks   eggs   hamburger
   candy   waffles   pork chops
   pretzels   orange juice   potato
   potato chips   cereal   chicken

B. Answers will vary.

C. Answers will vary.

Page 34
A. Answers will vary.

B. Poems will vary.

Page 35
A. 1. b   2. a   3. a   4. b

B. Answers will vary.

Page 36
Deserts get very little rainfall. It takes special
kinds of animals and plants to survive in such
a harsh climate. But many do. The camel can
go for a long time without drinking water. For
this reason, Bedouin people ride them as they
make their way through the desert. If you are
looking for water in a desert, you might be
happy to find a cactus This fleshy desert
plant holds water. If you're lucky enough to
find an oasis in the desert, you'll probably find
water there, too.

Page 37
Answers will vary.

Pages 38–39
A. 1. blend into
   2. protects
   3. Arctic fox and snowshoe hare
   4. disguise

B. Answers will vary but should convey the
   idea that being white helps them blend into
   their snowy surroundings, which helps
   them hunt their prey and also protects them
   from enemies.

C. Drawings and paragraphs will vary.

Pages 40–41
A. The students should circle the computer,
   light bulb, microwave, and refrigerator.

B. Stories will vary.

C. Benjamin Franklin lived at a time before
   electricity. He read and wrote by candlelight.
   However, Franklin was a person of great
   foresight He was one of the first people to
   experiment with electricity. Franklin lived and
   conducted his work in Philadelphia. In one of
   his experiments, he flew a homemade kite
   during a thunderstorm and proved that
   lightning is electricity. He harnessed lightning
   by using a lightning rod. What Franklin did
   was dangerous, but it laid the groundwork for
   many of the things we use today.

D. Articles will vary.

Page 42
A.–B. Answers will vary.

Page 43
Articles will vary.

Page 44
Answers will vary.

Page 45
Answers will vary.

Page 46
Letters will vary.